DENOUNCE!
Creating Awareness on Domestic Violence Through Translation
Sobreviví/I Survived

SILVANA MARCONI

Introduction
DR. GIADA BIASETTI

Translated by

Sasha Bent
Steven Boyd
Stephanie Castillo
Julio Chavez
Emilee Kirby

Sruthi Medicherla
Carragan Moody
Francesca Santander
Tania Satizabal
Hollie Swanson

Nathan Urioste

PUBLISHING

ISBN: 978-1-941416-35-8 (paperback)
ISBN: 978-1-941416-36-5 (eBook)
LCCN: 2023937248

P.R.A. Publishing
P.O. Box 211701
Martinez, Georgia 30917, USA
www.prapublishing.com

Interior and cover design by Medlar Publishing Solutions Pvt Ltd., India.
Cover Art *Lonely Life* digital artwork by Yogesh Sehgal.

Translated from Spanish *Sobreviví: Mi historia de violencia domestica*, Rumbo Editorial, 2020.

ACKNOWLEDGMENT

When I started with the idea of this project, I only had the need to talk about what I had to endure in my life years before. I never expected to write anything serious; though when I was younger, I had a diary and wrote some poems, obviously always spontaneously.

When I started writing, I realized that I needed help expressing myself. After lots of searching, I found an excellent literary workshop, which helped me enormously. Now I notice the change: I write with feeling; every word hurts me greatly; I have cried over and over again while rereading them.

I am profoundly thankful to my literature professor for her help, patience, and guidance … I also want to give thanks to my family, because every Saturday afternoon I went to the Literary Workshop and left them at home; very patiently, my husband gave up one of our favorite times, Saturday afternoons drinking *mate*, to take me there and bring me back. I also can't forget about my psychologist. I had a hard time remembering and I really didn't recall much. She helped me break that mental block and dig deeper into those vague images in my mind. I was amazed at this, but she explained to me that the mind protects us so that we can proceed with our lives.

Last but not least, I want to thank Joaquín Toyos, a law student, who took the time to read my draft with lots of interest in the topic and for the prologue he wrote.

I am forever grateful to all of you.

FORWARD

When Silvana asked me to write the prologue for her book, in addition to giving me immense pleasure, I noticed that at the same time she was experiencing violence in her home, the Uruguayan parliament approved the Law on Domestic Violence (Law 17.514). As fate would have it, that same year, this law would change her life forever, and it would give society the legal framework needed to protect its integrity.

She was not the only one with this story, many women and in many cases men in our country had similar stories. For many years, the nation had been carrying this problematic and impactful burden that affected our society and could no longer be ignored. Women were dying as a result of this problem; families were completely shattered.

Based on these occurrences, Law 17.514 was created with an endless number of principles designed to placate the problem of violence that affects the homes of many families. In the first place, although it seems strange to us, it was the first time that domestic violence was defined, designating it as: "physical abuse, psychic or emotional abuse, sexual abuse, and financial abuse", each with its respective definition.

The policy determines that the courts would deal with this topic differently and that the magistrate's courts in the interior have jurisdiction regarding Domestic Violence matters. It tries to equate the system to a criminal problem (without prejudice towards the crimes that fall in said system).

An article of the law that we rarely understand and is important to identify in this prologue (since it was decisive in Silvana's life and is fundamental for any person who is in this terrible situation and cannot escape) is Article 8: "Any person who becomes aware of an act of domestic violence, must inform the proper judge, who should take the measures deemed appropriate (…). The judge, officially or at the request of the Public Prosecutor's office may call third parties to trial."

Although the following and all the articles that make up this part of the law are important and necessary, one believes that the authority the policy grants us in the Article in question is decisive in contributing to the elimination of this harmful problem in our society.

When faced with this problem, people, to a great extent, are deaf, mute, and/or blind. Usually, no one heard, saw, and least of all will speak about the issue. It is everyone's responsibility to end this dilemma. Everyone is to blame when another woman dies because of this, and we are all responsible when we can save someone from a bad ending.

As readers of this story will realize, Silvana's story could've ended much sooner if someone had decided to report the aggressor. For example, the mother-in-law that never reported it, or the emergency room doctor she desperately turned to for help who did not care. Numerous things could've happened, but didn't.

Silvana's ending could've been different, perhaps worse, with an ending no one wants to imagine. But destiny decided otherwise. Instead, she got out, she succeeded and transformed her home into an exceptional family. She continued with her English classes; she keeps making progress in her job as a secretary, and today she feels strong and eager to share her story with society. Her story is impactful, dramatic, and strong and, as readers, we begin to feel hooked, so much so that we want to intervene and help the "Silvana" character. It is an exceptional true story that reflects a dramatic phenomenon that families in any socio-economic class can experience. It reaches us all equally, and it affects us in the same way.

We hope that this story will help the great number of men and women who are going through this painful situation.

Joaquín Toyos

INTRODUCTION

Beyond teaching a language and culture, my objective as a Spanish Professor is to allow students to develop their own frames of knowledge, engage in critical thinking, expand their arguments and interpretations, be creative, and make connections to and beyond the work of the class. I give students the opportunity to develop professionalism and give them tangible evidence of their knowledge and skill. The experiential learning projects I incorporate in my classes are crucial for students, and I am always willing to take the time to lay the groundwork, to coach and mentor the students through the process, and then act as editor, ensuring that the final product is of professional quality. One example of such an experiential learning project that is dear to my heart is the translation from Spanish into English of the book *Sobreviví: Mi historia de violencia doméstica* by Uruguayan author Silvana Marconi.

During Spring 2022, my students in Spanish 4600 (Introduction to Spanish/English Translation) translated Silvana Marconi's book into English. The topic of the book focuses on the author's experience with domestic violence and the objective of the translation project was to reach a wider audience to increase awareness on this important topic. As part of the project, I also organized a virtual event that took place on April 22nd, 2022 where students discussed their experience with the translation process and engaged in a thought-provoking conversation with the author and the publisher, Lucinda Clark from PRA Publishing. Some of the other invited special guests included Aimee Hall from SafeHomes Domestic Violence Center, Julie Kneuker (Augusta University's Title IX coordinator), Dr. Seretha Williams (Chair of the Department of English and World Languages), Dean Kim Davies from Pamplin College of Arts, Humanities, and Social Sciences, and Frank Iodice from Articoli Liberi. This project and collaboration led to many more interviews, projects, and presentations focusing on the translation process, translation as a profession, and the art of teaching translation. The project gained international recognition through Silvana Marconi and the many interviews she carried out in Uruguay and Italy.

To say I am proud of my students is an understatement. Sasha Bent, Steven Boyd, Stephanie Castillo, Julio Chavez, Emilee Kirby, Sruthi Medicherla, Carragan Moody, Francesca Santander, Tania Satizabal, Hollie Swanson, and Nathan Urioste did an extraordinary job completing this project and all its different facets. They were given a task that was not easy to complete. This project gave them the opportunity to apply what they had learned in class, it showcased their full potential, it took them out of their comfort zone, and it gave them a sense of what it means to be a professional translator. They worked in groups and selected a group leader in charge of making sure the deadlines were met and that there was consistency within the translation. Teamwork (knowing how to translate and solve problems as a team) was part of the learning process and one of the objectives of the project. The groups were also tasked with participating in a virtual discussion designed to share the challenges faced during the translation process, ask questions, and provide suggestions on how to improve the translation. After completing the first draft, students peer-reviewed the translations by checking spelling mistakes, punctuation, accuracy, naturalness, and consistency. Once their review and my review were completed, students turned in their final draft, which was reviewed once more. This semester-long project gave students the opportunity to understand translation as a profession and experience the complexities of the process. Moreover, they were able to connect with the content and increase their awareness on topics such as domestic violence.

The discussion on domestic violence is of utmost importance. Unfortunately, when this happened to Silvana over 20 years ago in Uruguay, the term "domestic violence" wasn't something people spoke about freely. Organizations focused on helping victims of domestic violence did not exist yet in Uruguay and Silvana's situation was met often with indifference from doctors, police officers, friends, and loved ones. This is the reason why this project and the message Silvana's story conveys is so important. Nowadays, these kinds of organizations do exist and, although still challenging, it is easier to get help when dealing with domestic violence. The book's power lies in its capacity to send a message to everyone to speak up and report the violence. Through her words and her experience, she gives people the courage to get the justice they deserve and save themselves from a potentially deadly situation. One particular quote from the book comes to mind and perfectly reflects the power of Silvana's words. To finalize this introduction, I would like to include this quote in three languages in order to highlight the power of the book and the importance of transmitting this message to various cultures. We need to increase awareness on this topic and inspire people to come forward by using translation as a powerful tool that breaks barriers and reaches a wider audience. Here is the Spanish, Italian, and English version of Silvana's powerful message:

(Spanish Original) "Denuncia y defiende tu derecho a la Vida. Denuncia y sostén tu sobrevivencia; y si aún así no te sientes fuerte para denunciarlo, puedes acudir a mí sin duda, pero por favor, la vida es sagrada, solo Dios o la Divinidad en que creas puede llevarnos cuando nos llegue la hora, no un cobarde que abusa de nosotras; ¡DENUNCIA!, por todas las mujeres que han sido asesinadas, por todas las mujeres que hemos resucitado, y por Ti misma, porque todas estamos en Ti."

(Italian translation by Frank Iodice) "Denuncia e difendi il tuo diritto alla vita. Denuncia e preserva la tua sopravvivenza. E se non ti senti ancora forte per farlo, io sono qui per te. Ma per favore, la vita è sacra, solo Dio o la divinità in cui credi ci può venire a prendere quando arriva l'ora, non un codardo che abusa di noi. Denuncia! Per tutte le donne che sono state assassinate, per tutte le donne salvate dalla morte, e per te stessa, perché tutte siamo in te."

(English translation by Dr. Biasetti's students) "Denounce and defend your right to Live. Denounce and support your survival; and if you still do not feel strong enough to denounce it, do not hesitate to reach out to me. But, please, life is sacred, only God or the Divinity you believe in can take us when the time comes, not a coward who abuses us; DENOUNCE! Do it for all the women who have been murdered, for all the women we have resurrected, and for Yourself, as we are all a part of You."

Dr. Giada Biasetti, Editor
Associate Professor of Spanish,
Augusta University

ME, TODAY

My name is Silvana. I am 39 years old, and I live in Montevideo, more specifically in the Nuevo París neighborhood. I was born, raised, and spent some of the darkest and most wonderful moments of my life here.

It's a pretty impoverished neighborhood, but the solidarity of my neighbors taught me to love it as it is: a symbol of productivity from other decades, with its factories and tanneries now closed; a place that holds all the golden leaves of so many resilient trees, still standing strong even though the autumns and winters dishevel their foliage; a nurturing place where you can smell the simple joy of children.

Because of this, I am convinced that even if they offered to move me to Pocitos, Carrasco, or another more charming area, I wouldn't think twice: I was born here and here I will stay.

I am an English teacher. I've been teaching since I was 17. I also work as a secretary at an important law firm downtown.

I have been married for three years. My husband is in the military, and I met him online when he was deployed in the Republic of Congo … destiny works in mysterious ways … but that is another story.

I have two children: a 12-year-old girl and a 14-year-old boy.

We love animals. We have four dogs: a Great Dane, a Saint Bernard, and two Weiner dogs. We all live in peace … especially me … far away from the torture endured a decade ago, now distant from it and stronger because of it.

They say that when someone has been in Hell but has managed to come back from it, he or she has pledged to carry out some kind of mission. Mine is to tell the story of when I lived in that space, in that infernal territory that I can only now embody in words.

I took too long to decide that it was time to fulfill my promise. My psyche was not motivated to show my scars of human brutality, those that always linger behind those blows shamefully healed by the body.

Surviving domestic violence means a lot more than saving your skin and your questionable sanity. I realized this when the words of this book began to burn my mouth, my eyes, and this hand that was writing "Me, Today" …

The burning had begun in the bus, one afternoon when I returned from work. I had been thinking of so many women beaten, riddled, stabbed, burned … so many mourned … so many unprotected … so many forgotten.

I was thinking that I was alive—thank God—that my family was waiting for me, that I was remembered by friends, that I was able to create projects like this one, and that it had been on my mind for years. "There is no place for fear when one has these privileges," I grumbled. And I listened to my own advice.

From the bottom of her non-transferable pain, not yet convinced of my drastic resolution, the former victim whispered to me: "Will you dare proclaim authorship with your full name?" "What if someone gets offended?" "What if he takes revenge?"

"I don't care," I replied. "Now I am strong; I have a Voice now and I will make it run among the silence of the cowards so that one of them, named Ricardo, knows that I, Silvana Marconi, am not the jagged torn peel of an apple that is later thrown out, deformed and fetid, into the trash; I am a nest of Life, I am the sacred seed, I am the millenary heart of the apple."

3

THE FIRST DATE

Since I was a little girl, I dreamed of having a family, a happy one, obviously, and for me, that meant marriage and having children, specifically a boy.

In high school I had many friends; most of them smoked and would offer some to me but I never accepted, because I was resolute that my children would be healthy, and I stuck to that.

During this time, I had many boyfriends but none of the relationships were serious.

I loved to go dancing, even though there were always problems, partly because of my selfishness; my friends loved dancing to cumbia and I to Madonna, even now.

I had been a fan before: I spent afternoons with my friend pretending to be "paquitas" and "xuxas"[1]; and a while after that I was dazzled by Axl Rose's legs as they moved to the beat of "Don't Cry," and I even wore his bandana. This was unusual as I preferred the comfort of my jeans and my sneakers; fashion didn't matter much to me.

At 21, I ended a relationship that grew weak with time, and I was single for months. I used to accompany my mom on her errands around the neighborhood.

She frequently visited a very popular produce stand. Everyone shopped there. A man and his mother were the owners. He was a tall man, with light brown hair and brown eyes. It was a color that was not too attractive for my taste at that time when I did not doubt that only light eyes revealed the soul.

But his eyes captivated me because his look resembled that of a helpless child. Although he had the darkest fingernails that I have ever seen ("because of work," I repeated to myself), I did not hold myself back in asking a neighbor about him.

---

[1] The terms "paquitas" and "xuxas" come from a Brazilian children's television show called *Xuxa* that aired in 1993. This show was hosted by a woman named Xuxa Meneghel. The dancers were called "paquitas" in the original version and "pixies" in the English version.

She found out what she could: he was 24 years old, didn't have a girlfriend, was very family-oriented, and most importantly, he didn't smoke.

When she agreed to be the middleman, my mother warned that I wouldn't tolerate him because I was very picky with neatness and "those dirty fingernails!"

On a Saturday night on March 20th, 1999, we had our first date. My neighbor and other people were slyly waiting for him to show up; I was on the corner, and I knew that he'd come in his truck.

We went all over Montevideo, from La Barra de Santa Lucía to Parque Rodó.

"Are you hungry?", he asked me suddenly halfway through. Tell me and I will go to my shop to find some bananas. I must have said no because it would've been unforgettable to have peeled bananas on a first date.

THE COURTSHIP

We continued going out: on Saturdays until the early morning; on weekdays we saw each other for a short time or we would speak for hours on the phone.

As the months passed things changed. He started dropping me off at home by midnight. I wasn't happy seeing him for such a short amount of time, but he said that he wanted to go to sleep early because he was tired from the heavy work week. I didn't argue with him, I tried to understand and not berate him.

THE ENGAGEMENT

In our second year of dating, we decided to get engaged and buy the rings. My family was aware of this, but Ricardo wasn't motivated to inform his family, specifically his mother. She was a short stubby lady with very little hair and a friendly face that no one suspected could hold even a drop of ill-intent. She was a desensitized lady on the inside due to working in the fields as a teen and doing hard labor in the Mercado Modelo.

He was so reluctant to bring up the topic to his mom, that he begged me to say that I was paying for the gold rings with my card.

It felt odd to me, but I did not question his actions … (My husband was that brave, and I was that blind!)

Either way, his mother was angry for not being notified ahead of time to celebrate such a special event.

Perhaps the ring woke up my dormant intuition. It was a Saturday after he dropped me off at my parent's home at midnight.

Fifteen minutes after he left, it occurred to me to make a romantic call, but his mother replied that he was not home.

I didn't think it was an accident; my body froze in an instant; the world fell apart and I with it. I ran and ran. I wanted to check that the truck was not stopped in front of his house.

"Where are you? Are you with another? Are you in some sleezy place? My doubt has been eating away at me for a long time. Are you faithful to me? Where, where are you? Why isn't my love, my dedication, and my understanding enough? Don't you realize that I'm not fat, that I bike and go on long walks, that I take care of my hair and curls, my face …" Out in the open, and for two hours, I repeated the complaint as if he were in front of me. Until he arrived … It took him a while to get out of the car: he was putting on his ring.

A few days later I forgave him. Oh, God, today I wonder why! There were many clues indicating that a time of pain and suffering was very near, but we women believe that our love is omnipotent. And so, I also felt this way when I decided not to consider myself defeated.

A SMALL HOUSE
FOR THE HAPPY FAMILY

Three years had passed, and I wanted to formalize the relationship, I wanted us to live together. I suggested it to him, and he agreed, but he never actively looked for a house. So, I went through the neighborhood, looked at every house that was available for rent, took down telephone numbers, addresses, and real estate agencies, and, though I was super excited to tell him about my efforts, his continued disinterest was very frustrating for me.

Then I thought that there was a way I could do it without having to consult him and that it would relieve some frustration.

I was already 24 years old; I was not willing to wait any longer to become a mother; despite his cowardice, a decision had to be made. This is how it happened: I got pregnant right away.

It was an out-of-wedlock pregnancy because he continued to live in his house and I in mine, and we would see each other as always: at night or we would go out for a while on Saturday and Sunday afternoons when I would go to his house.

My mother was the first to know the news and she was thrilled. While I was unwilling to tell my father, I asked my mother to help me. One day when he gave me a ride in his car, he said "So I'm going to be a grandfather?" He gave me a kiss. It was a very touching moment.

I was also the one to tell Ricardo's mother. I was not close enough to his father to tell him, but he was a friendly and well-spoken gentleman. My now ex-mother-in-law did not want to convey the news to him because she felt that it was our responsibility.

One winter afternoon, when the siblings-in-law were also present drinking *mate* and watching television, our opportunity came. My stomach was very noticeable even though I wore large sweatshirts.

We entered together and when I said, "We have something very important to say," my brave boyfriend locked himself in the bathroom. With my words stuck in my throat,

I waited for him for a few minutes, but I had to face the situation on my own.

Later, when everyone congratulated me and gave me kisses, out came my trembling boyfriend.

I gained 62 pounds during my pregnancy since I had preeclampsia. My fiancée would avoid me during the week. When we were alone, I came to the conclusion that my belly disgusted him, and on the seventh month, he told me that he didn't want to make love because he was sickened by the fatness of my belly.

It hurt me a lot ... but I couldn't force him to love the nest where his son was growing.

Like a bag of merchandise thrown mercilessly on the truck bed of the Fiorino that they used for work, that's how I would travel on Sundays when we went out; his mother, so smug, in the passenger seat, and I, without any complaint, enduring the rocking and swaying caused by traffic; It was enough for them to lift my leg to get down: that was their weekly good deed.

We did not get to settle on the small house of my dreams while waiting for my son. I felt as if I was out in the cold, but, close to the birth of my child, my now ex-mother-in-law commented that she had bought a spacious piece of land for all of us to live in: we would be living there together, in an old house to remodel, while she and her husband would build another one in the back.

When she invited me to visit the place, I was overwhelmed by great loneliness. Perhaps it was because the former owners of the demolished house were an elderly couple who had been confined to only two rooms. Today I think it was a kind of premonition. But Ricardo's mother's immediate decision to hire construction workers (including my father) won over this feeling.

And I even believed that I was part of that project because she invited me to choose many of the materials.

The ceramics and sanitary fixtures for the bathroom were bought in pink, my favorite color; I also opted for green ceramics with white details, as well as curtains over the large windows resembling those of a lovely winter garden.

Because of that unexpected involvement, and the happiness my son would bring me, the prolonged stay with my parents became more tolerable.

MY LITTLE GARDEL

The doctors had established the birth to take place on March 20th, 2002, a date that surprised me because it was the anniversary of the first date of the baby's mother and father.

But the child was born the next day: my blood pressure was very high when I was hospitalized.

Because the child was a boy, the father named him; it seemed fair to me since I would've been the one naming the child if it had been a girl.

What is odd is that I still can't express how I felt when I saw him and held him for the first time. But I do remember the sound of his crying because he couldn't suckle enough, and the nurses took him. They returned him to me the next morning: I could not forget the funny hairstyle he had. It looked like Gardel's.

THE PREMIERE

A lthough our house was still being remodeled, the three of us moved in by May. My ex-mother-in-law still lived three blocks away.

The first months passed without issue, but certain parts of his behavior just weren't ideal. Even though I understood very well that we couldn't have lunch together because of his work, he also had dinner with his mother and then came home just to sleep.

When I would ask him about it, as an answer he would just give me a look, the coldest of looks, and nothing else.

Within three months came my first son, the first grandson, and the first nephew—with curly hair and precious eyes just as black—a giant baby, adored by everyone.

It was a good time to baptize him and celebrate with a little reunion at home.

But I worried about the moment when my husband and my parents would be under the same roof for the first time.

The relationship between them wasn't anything more than "hi" and "bye," given that my now ex-partner had never stepped foot into my parents' house; they met him on the sidewalk on any given day.

In the span that my father worked as a construction worker, they may have exchanged two words back and forth and nothing more.

In any case, it was a peaceful encounter, and my son felt as good in the church as he did at home.

In reality, he was a quiet baby, so much so that he stayed by my side in his stroller without any interruption while I taught class.

One afternoon, after my last student had left, we got ready to go visit my father-in-law who was already in the terminal stage of lung cancer.

A little after arriving, he passed away. I took my son to my parents' house and came back to help in any way possible.

The whole neighborhood was there, having the same painful feeling of grief the family was experiencing, as this man had gained the affection of the whole neighborhood.

Collective pain is very touching, and rare. The only person who didn't cry, nor did he cry in any other moment, was the father of my child, and he never wanted to talk about it.

A LANGUAGE WITHOUT WORDS

One night, I woke up in the early morning and he wasn't in bed. I got up and found him sitting on the couch in the living room. I leaned over and asked him what was wrong, but as there was no answer, I insisted.

He lifted his head, looked at me, got on his feet, stopped, pushed me onto the couch, and punched me. I shouted in pain, and then he unleashed a continuous barrage of punches.

I managed to cover my face to protect my eyes as I use contact lenses. When he got tired, he went to lay down …

I froze up, feeling as if my muscles were reacting inch by inch to the punches; not one piece of my mind could understand why he had acted this way. Like an animal.

The profound silence made me realize that I hadn't heard my baby. When I went into his room, I found him peacefully sleeping, and a sense of relief washed over my body. I returned to the couch, as I didn't feel like going to bed; it was when sleep overcame me that I went into our bedroom. He was sleeping like a saint.

Luckily it was already wintertime, and the next morning my clothes hid the bruises.

I told no one what had happened. I was ashamed. It had been a long time since I'd seen my friends, each one of them already settled into their lives. We would call each other every once in a while, but I knew that if I went looking for them, they would be loyal.

But I really didn't want to mention it, not even to myself; I thought that this was just an isolated incident, caused by the pain of the loss of his father, that once it passed, he would reflect and would never do it again, that there would be no reason to worry …

A couple of days went by, and I started to believe I overreacted because everything had gone back to normal.

We even went for a drive, with my mother-in-law, of course. She was riding in the front as usual, on the passenger's side, and I, obviously, had to sit in the back, although this time it wasn't in the truck bed because it was an actual car. It didn't matter if I had my child or not, my place was, undeniably, in the back. If his mother wasn't with us, we never went out alone.

One night, he came home from work, completely silent, and he wouldn't even look at me. I was cooking, or trying to cook, as it wasn't my strong suit, but I never gave up.

With a tomato in my hand, I spoke to him, but since he did not respond. I went up to him and asked him what was wrong.

He grabbed me by the arms, threw me against the wall, and hit me with such fury that if I hadn't screamed so loud, enough to have the neighbors hear me, he would have never let me go; this angered him even more, I could see it in his eyes.

I managed to get away and tried to hit him with the tomato, but I missed, and it smashed against the glass of the window. Enraged, he overpowered me once again with his fists that felt as hard as rocks; I didn't defend myself. I couldn't beat him. My body and soul were just so tired, hopeless. They were dead.

The blame came after. Entire weeks passed without him saying anything to me or even looking at me, as if I deserved these cruel punishments.

I don't know how many times these violent acts occurred; the scars were enough to prove what my memory couldn't.

The night I left; I knew how many times it had occurred and I couldn't let it happen anymore.

I bundled up my son and I went to my parents' house. I did not tell them the truth; I argued that it had been weeks since he had talked to me and that I had no idea why.

My abuser called my parents to explain the reason that I had left the house; I had become a rebel.

He also asked to talk to me; he calmly suggested that I come home, and he convinced me.

He and his mother were waiting for me. We had what appeared to be a well-intentioned conversation. However, it took him over a week to break his silence.

A SECOND CHANCE

Before my son turned one, I had to undergo a small gynecological operation, which didn't require hospitalization but did require general anesthesia.

My mother was with me the whole time. My abuser did not show up or call—honestly, it did not surprise me …

I was discharged the next day. So that I would not overwork myself, my son stayed with my parents.

My abuser was at home that afternoon, but he was his usual self: mute. It was very cold; we were in the middle of winter.

I asked him to reach for a blanket for me. He approached with a terrible look on his face, so much so that I assumed it was another beating (but what I got was worse). He came even closer and said to me, "Why didn't you die during the operation?"

DENOUNCE!

My head spun—Was this man really hoping for my death? An unknown kind of pain crushed me as if I had been put in a straitjacket.

Weeks passed. Almost nothing had changed except that when he decided to acknowledge me, he demanded that I leave the house because his mother urged him to.

I replied that it was impossible for me, that I had nowhere to go, that my parents could not house two people in a small place.

One night the tone and reason for the request changed.

He had come home from work in a very bad mood; his face was almost distorted. And when the fight began, he dared to say that it was not his mother who demanded it, but it was because I bothered him. And to confirm that thought, he dragged me to the bathroom and threw me on the floor so he could destroy me more comfortably.

Under his stone fists and thick work shoes, I actually believed that the death he spoke about in that conversation was very close, very close …

Did death itself pity me that night?

When I could, I sat on the floor. The pink tile that I had so eagerly chosen for my "home" was freezing, and that coldness hurt me more than the newly inflicted wounds. It was difficult for me to stand up, but I did.

I was in the living room and he came in. I felt panicked: I knew I couldn't take any more blows. When he leaned me against the wall I couldn't breathe. But, very softly he said in my ear: "What did I do? What did I do? Let's go to bed. We can fix this in bed."

THE SCHEME OF INDIFFERENCE

T he next day after that beating, I called a friend and told her everything; she immediately came to my house and accompanied me to the Aquiles Lanza polyclinic, around the corner from my house, to be seen by a doctor, and with the medical certification, file a police report.

I think that was the protocol back then. I waited my turn and the doctor helped me, I told her what happened, and she made me undress. She said, "These blows are not fresh, they are not recent, so I can't give you any medical certification."

I couldn't believe it. I didn't respond, I got dressed as quickly as possible and left. I felt lost …

THE TRANSFORMATION
OF THE HOUSE

I never had a house key. My abuser thought his was enough.

At first, he would throw it through the bathroom window when he would leave for the market at dawn.

But one morning, I didn't find it there; I had to go out and hang clothes that I had washed, and even though I had looked for it meticulously throughout the entire house, I still couldn't find it. So, I called him on the phone, so that he could tell me what happened.

As if nothing, he told me that he would give it back to me when he felt like it, and in the meantime, I should make do.

That day, my son and I spent the day locked away in the house until 5 in the afternoon, when he arrived with a sarcastic laugh and a triumphant stance. It was obvious that he felt that the situation had been exemplary: he was in charge.

Days later, his mother took it upon herself to tell me that Ricardo's discomfort was motivated by the fact that strangers were entering the house, that is, my students, and because of that it would be best that I stop working.

The illusion of forming a happy family had not been extinguished; I realized that when I accepted her advice.

I do not know how I did not even realize that a plan to isolate me had been laid out and my alienation was progressing in strides.

He no longer left me money for groceries, he did not bring any food, and I could not go to the store to buy anything because I was denied access to it. I insisted on asking why, and blows were the usual response.

But one day I rebelled: I bundled up my son and showed up at the store; I was determined to get vegetables to make a stew. I put the stroller at the entrance, but I did not go in. He was shocked and motionless. Then he came over to me to mumble that he would come home with vegetables when he had time.

I believed him, then I went to my parents' house and left my son there; I knew that they would look after him, like his father should.

I headed home; I knew that he would go crazy if he did not find me there, and not because he missed me, but because he would lose control if the house was left unattended. He had already told me on an extremely hot summer day, "It's so hot and the house is right where the sun is blazing. Go back there now!"

Any situation was conducive to damaging my self-esteem, and so I remember recurring phrases like "Your parents don't love you," "I'll kill your hunger,"] "You've stayed disgustingly fat after the pregnancy" ... Phrases that seemed to have been pinned to the walls because they resonated day after day in that prison.

I was waiting for the ingredients until late, but that night, I ate a stew of blows. When he returned, he gave me the beating of my life. It was the worst: kicks, punches, insults, reprimands (that I was forbidden to enter the store, that I had disobeyed him, that his mother was angry because of it).

I cried, screamed, pleaded that I could not endure it any longer. Meanwhile, I heard my mother-in-law's footsteps outside, to the point that I thought that she would come in to stop him. A delusion of mine, evidently. A hallucination that repeated itself the next morning.

When I came across her in the space we shared, and believing that out of gender solidarity she would pity my situation, I asked her if she had heard her son's fierce attack the night before.

Calmly, she said that she did not notice anything, and walked away without the slightest worry.

She was the second woman to refuse to help me, and this repeated indifference destroyed me.

I fell into a deep depression: I did not feel the desire for anything.

Little by little, I was feeling more and more cornered: The residents of the neighborhood were adding to this, specifically those who made purchases through the old credit system.

In order to appear more trustworthy, they approached the abuser or his mother to tell them that the child had cried in the street or that he had sneezed ... they reported any action from the little boy that seemed interesting to them in order to ensure the provision of their food.

What a paradox! We, his family, were starved; they, on the other hand, were granted even the benefit of familiarity. They would immediately call me after they were informed, trying to intimidate me for my lack of care, which was publicly seen by their faithful clientele.

Another degree of complicity weighed heavily on my paralysis: this was an anonymous conspiracy. So much so that I was avoiding even the smallest and most innocent daily routines.

One time, for example, my sister suggested that I go to a large grocery store to buy my son a gift; I hesitated to go, because I knew that if I went out, I was going to have problems with my abuser, in addition to fearing some dizzy spells like the ones I had been suffering from.

To reassure me, she called Public Health, explaining to them my situation and my symptoms; they responded saying that they did not seem serious and that it was most likely because I was pregnant. The service at the time was so inefficient and apathetic!

Anyway, I took the risk of more blows and went with her, but I was not calm, I felt like a robot in the middle of those shelves full of options; I wanted to return home immediately, I was scared that my abuser would not find me; I really couldn't stand even the thought of the blows that day.

We ended up buying an inflatable pool, which was not the perfect gift that my sister had set out to buy for her nephew.

WHEN HUNGER DEVOURS

My nutrition had been suffering for a long time, even though my grandmother tried to make up for my husband's abandonment and would come loaded with food from the supermarket every morning; sometimes I would put her at ease by going to eat at my parents' house, but that caused me a lot of shame and I hardly took a bite.

My weakness reached such an extent that I chose to stay in bed permanently; I was so dizzy that I could not stand up.

I believe my ex-mother-in-law got scared so she came to my bedroom with a cup of soup. I hesitated to accept it; I was afraid that it was poisoned. But the comforting and homey smell that came from the cup captivated me and spurred my appetite, so I took a risk and desperately ate it. I imagine she brought it to me without anyone noticing.

Anyhow, I almost never went out during the week; at most, I would take my son to the botanical garden and from there we would go to my parents' house, where we felt safe.

Sundays and Mondays, however, I dared to stay at home, only so my son could have contact with his father's family; I did not want to fill him with resentment.

He wouldn't notice me locking myself into the room for the entire day, the only space where my presence was not repulsive to anyone.

More days of fasting went by, and it was well controlled, even though in the eyes of everyone else they were very good at pretending that everything at home was normal. It was very telling.

My birthday is in December, and I have always thought that the passage of life should be celebrated. So, immersed in my naivety, I still hoped that my husband would call a truce, a truce that never came.

Instead, he stopped talking to me a week before, although he did not go to work that day and went to his mother's house.

I tried to act as if the spirit of festivities was still there, and I dedicated myself to cleaning the house thoroughly; I even prepared a sweet and simple cake with a little bit of flour and other leftover ingredients that were in the cupboard because my parents had told me that they would come by to visit. I had no idea that my mother-in-law would show up because she hadn't even looked at me when I was hanging clothes in the back.

I was sure that my friends would not visit me; they had already called me, and I avoided the possibility of them seeing me in the state that I was in.

At night my parents arrived and within a few minutes the act began: "Oh Silvana, I did not know you did not cook or buy anything to celebrate! That can't be! Let's go buy some sandwiches!" said my mother-in-law, but neither she nor the predator had the dignity to bring a candle for the cake. What actors! And my parents were a part of the cheerful performance.

As strange as it may seem, the act allowed me to begin to become aware of what was happening and I secretly promised myself that, from now on, I would not give anyone the power to minimize me in such a way.

I had given him permission to reduce me to nothing. I had been responsible for my hunger, my confinement, my physical pain, my vulnerability, my loneliness …

However, a brief understanding of that surface-level truth is not enough; it takes a lot of strength to make it a reality.

RED LIGHT

As my baby grew older, he caught colds more often. His pediatrician initially recommended an oral vaccine but later decided that it was a good idea to remove his tonsils. He recovered quickly. His father then considered that it was better for him to be with him during the day, at his grandmother's house, behind ours.

While living together, our son started to develop unpleasant behaviors, acquired by imitating his father, like eating his boogers, for example, a disgusting habit that Ricardo had no shame carrying out in public.

But I was greatly surprised when one afternoon I sat on a bench away from the meeting held by "this sacred family"; they were drinking *mate* and talking.

Suddenly, I heard my mother-in-law say to my son, "Throw those rocks at her," a command that the child immediately obeyed.

As the shower of stones fell on me—which even broke a window—his naive insults calling me "Ugly, ugly, ugly" tore at my soul.

My mother warned me that I was beginning to lose my son, which was heartbreaking, especially since my child's violence was increasing day by day; he went as far as throwing anything he could reach at me—in line with his father's new efforts to alienate me.

Since he thought I was responsible for the glass the boy broke, he tried to throw me out of the house, and he used the most diverse techniques for his purpose. At first, he started routinely calling my parents at night, after our child fell asleep, and he told them that, since I was "rebelling," it was up to them to "Straighten me out."

And it was true, I was openly rebelling. I was no longer silent around him and my tone was more defiant, even if a storm of blows would come later.

My parents used to come around the house to convince me of the benefits of being docile: "What did you do, child!" "Come on, Silvana, work on yourself a little bit", "You have to pull yourself together. Your husband and your mother-in-law have money; there is no room for you and your son at home."

Then, he wanted to convince me that my son no longer loved me.

- When do you plan to leave? You don't seem to understand that no one here loves you, not even your son loves you! My mother does not want you to be here either.
- I'm not going to leave, I have no reason to leave, my son lives here, the family I've created.
- Your family lives a few blocks from here, and they do not love you! No one loves you; do you not realize that as soon as your son sees you, he throws stones at you for being a bad mother! You don't even know how to prepare a bottle for him. You are a bad mother!

Perhaps the blows are not as effective as the psychological abuse.

I was already going crazy. And on an alarmingly chilly night, I could not stand it anymore and I left. With my son. I wrapped him in a lot of wool clothing, put him in the stroller, and went directly to the police station.

Without mentioning the daily physical abuse (I did not have the famous medical certificate to report it as violence), I explained the situation to an officer.

We immediately got into a patrol car, and he asked me for my home address. On the way, I called my sister so that she could prepare a place for us to sleep at my parents' house.

The predator did not appear in front of the police, but his mother did. She told them that I was difficult, defiant, loudmouthed, lazy (because I only painted my nails), and wasteful.

To my surprise, the officer told her: "And what is the problem, ma'am, with her buying clothes? Do you want the woman to walk around naked?"

For the first time, I felt like someone was walking a mile in my shoes! And it was a man!

I gathered our clothes with great peace of mind. He stood there, upright, convinced we needed protection, and on a mission.

My father came to get us, but he did not ask anything. No one asked anything.

That night we slept in my grandmother's room.

For two days, we were at peace. On the third day, the predator called:

"Look what you did! Because of you, I spent the night at the police station."

LIBERATION

From then on, we were separated. He didn't send me money; once a week he would bring a crate of groceries with some potatoes, a carton of milk, two or three apples and a little pastry so that the boy could eat during the seven days.

We argued a lot during these brief encounters. I demanded more groceries and diapers but he insisted he wouldn't spend more.

One time he became so angry he busted the only carton of milk he had the dignity to bring, then screamed at me, "There you have it; it's dented like you; look what you did!" It was just by luck that no one was passing by. My son missed his father a lot; he cried so much he would spike a fever. We often visited the Emergency Room. The only comfort I could bring him was short-lived. To both of us, but for different reasons, it seemed like time was stolen: to him because

Sundays were the only days he saw his father; to me, because of the uncertainty, the helplessness, the failure, and the normalized pain in my body and soul, the family dream had already been hindered, or in other words, I felt a complex mix of blame, placed only on myself. I didn't even see the traffic light was red. I simply did another loop around the circle. We met by chance one day and agreed to talk the next day.

Around five years ago, we went to Prado. He didn't mention the beatings and he focused on his mother instead. He told me that she was the one who prohibited my entrance in the store because she thought I was stealing, that she was hysterical and old, and that we shouldn't pay attention to her. He promised to pick us up for dinner in a restaurant the next night. And he did it. Not only that night, but many nights in a row. There was romance in the air along with the beginning of a new courtship.

We spent months in that situation, up until when I told him that I wanted to live together again and that our son deserved to have a stable family. His only argument was, "My mom doesn't want you to live there." I thought waiting for him after closing the store would be a good strategy: she wouldn't find out and we could then continue to fix our relationship.

Unexpectedly, one day she told me I was allowed in the store and so I went in. I thought the situation would lead to a second chance. I continued believing in a second chance until one afternoon Ricardo told me not to go in because there were a lot of people in the store; I waited and waited until the number of customers in the store was close to none. I walked in and stood in the corner.

Not long after I sat in the corner, a girl, barely eighteen, stared at me with an angry look and yelled, "He, he is my boyfriend. He comes to my house every day. He is mine." As usual, "her boyfriend" disappeared, while his mom brought me downstairs so that the girl could leave the store. Days passed with no news. So, one day, I decided to go to his house. Right when I reached the front door, three unfamiliar people arrived: an older woman and two girls.

While he disappeared like a gust of wind, the older woman warned me to be careful. She explained that since about half a year ago he was dating her 14-year-old daughter and was welcomed into their family.

Of course, the boyfriend's mother was there to witness the entire thing. She also warned me we shouldn't drag her into the conversation because she didn't know anything.

Then, she told me to come into the house for an explanation on the situation. An explanation? There was no explanation needed, it was all crystal clear to me: Ricardo, with his hands on his head, desperately repeated "What a bad impression I made on that family!" I was of no importance, and neither was my son. Even less, the little girl that hadn't even turned fifteen-years old yet. He was a true predator, a perfect example of Uruguayan machismo.

Up until that moment, I believed that matters such as these—arguments between women, threats, abuse—belonged only amongst the poor and uncultured masses. I quickly learned that violence doesn't discriminate no matter your economic standing, your social standing, or your education. I also began to question why Life or God had burdened me with this hell I was going through. Was it my naivety—a part of my personality that as a child I was always told would be dangerous—or was I a result of the absence of education that should be given to women? Why me, why is this happening to me?

I tried to continue with my life and forget he existed. I began studying, perfecting my English, intent on concentrating on just those things. And on my son. It was a very painful time for me, that literally weighed on my soul.

On Sunday afternoons, they would pick up my son and bring him back Monday evening. When I would call to see how my son did overnight, his grandmother would cut me off. She would only speak to my mother.

One time his father answered the phone. To my surprise, he spoke to me kindly, calmly, without humiliating me and told me how my son was doing and what time he was planning to bring him back to me.

After two days he called again, he sounded sad. He invited me over one night for a chat. As a result of that night chatting, we decided to start working on us again. For both of us that meant confronting his mother.

SECOND CHANCE

Although the first couple days were peaceful, it was obvious from the start he struggled to free himself of the hold his mother had on him, even when it came to the smallest of things. In the store, if the *dulce de membrillo* ran out, he wouldn't replace it until she told him to.

My mom would often suggest that the unhealthy dependency would die when his mom did.

I could now enter the store and even work there. I was in charge of helping the customers and I loved it; I had started my classes again as well; my son had started to walk … All in all, I couldn't complain.

However, I still didn't like some of his behavior, like waking up without saying anything and immediately going to eat breakfast with his mom.

Anyway, waking up without being scared was a big step forward. Another improvement was telling me ahead of time that when we went out his mother would be sitting by him.

The absence of physical abuse allowed me to normalize the lack of communication and his occasional bad temper.

On the other hand, my performance at work improved thanks to Laura, one of my friends. I covered for her for three-months in a candy shop. I began teaching classes nearby and then at the house.

I had a lot of students, thank God, and that gave me strength.

But, soon things went back to how they were and he began to show his usual indifference; he didn't let me know when he was going out and the ghosts from his past infidelities began to creep up on me; jealousy could become my worst enemy.

The situation with the fourteen-year-old girl was very recent and the rumors continued to spread: "The car was parked in front of this or that motel"; "Oh, I saw your husband's car leaving El Prado the other night …"

It's sad to say that one time, on my way back home alone from a birthday party (because he never came with me anywhere), I saw him leaving El Prado with my own eyes and thought: "Now it's crystal clear."

THE QUALIFIED REPORTER

Since my now ex-mother-in-law hadn't finished renovating her house, more workers had to be hired. Among them was a construction worker who happened to be a resident in the neighborhood, was well known by my then mother-in-law, and was a loyal customer at the store. One night when I was home alone, someone knocked on the door and when I opened it, I met the well-known worker.

He came to ask for some sugar; I found it a bit strange as he had never approached me in this manner. But, anyway, I went to the kitchen to get some sugar and brought it to him.

I do not know how the conversation started, but he began to tell me that I was very pretty; that I did not have to put up with Ricardo; that it was in my interest to leave him; that finding a man who would treat me the way I deserved to be treated would be very easy; and that it would be his pleasure to be the one to do it, all I had to do was say the word.

I was totally shocked and even disgusted, so I asked him to leave and locked the door. I couldn't believe what had just happened … That man was about 35 years old, short, obese, and with brown skin.

The disgust I had for him grew to such an extent that, when my mother arrived, it was the first thing I told her. My wise mother interpreted it as a set-up by my ex-mother-in-law to manipulate her son by using a real situation and lead him to kick me out again.

My naivety had no limits, because I replied that I did not believe that she was capable of creating such an elaborate scheme.

As we were exchanging our thoughts, the schemer appeared.

Of course, she seemed horrified, tried to fire him, and advised me to put a lock on the door. In reality, her actions were the opposite of what she said, because every time she prepared a family dinner or had a tea party with *mate*, the construction worker was one of the first guests to be invited. I would lock myself in the house.

I had explained to her various times how I felt about the worker's presence, but it was obvious that it was a new trick to separate us. And it started to work.

The arguments and fights became more and more frequent; everything started to bother him again, even the way I hung up my clothes.

One Sunday, everyone decided to go to the Piedras Blancas fair. I had never been to it, but Ricardo decided that I wouldn't go; he yelled at me like crazy and demanded that I stay in the house because I did not deserve to go due to my behavior from the previous day.

And that's how things went. During all that time, I was thinking and thinking, but I couldn't remember doing anything out of the norm. Later that day, I realized that it had been an excuse to alienate me from the family and a way to make me believe once again that it was all my fault.

Was it a mother-son plot? Which of the two was more mentally sick? In reality, I didn't even realize it was a triangle and that I was one of the vertices because I was living that moment as if I were strapped to a propeller going round and round without being able to stop. I should've realized after witnessing some of his behavior when we were intimate; he tried not to make any sound as if we were secretly seeing each other.

I didn't even pay any attention to it when in one of the occasions I had the guts to ask why we were being so sneaky. His answer was, "My mom doesn't want us having intercourse."

Perhaps it was to watch how we would behave that she booked a camping trip to Treinta y Tres, which I was invited to.

We could also add the fact that she was sure that her grandson wouldn't go without me.

The idea of it was not appealing to me at all but I had no intention of causing another argument either. My headphones would definitely give me a way to escape that family nucleus that so ardently rejected me.

One morning, they decided to cross the river on a raft and I sat at the edge of the river to enjoy nature and some good music. I didn't feel alone at any moment.

I WAS NOT ALONE

Getting to Montevideo was a relief. In a house in the city, there is no grass, no threat of rain, and no moths, which have always terrified me.

But the relief didn't last long. Getting back into routine meant having the time to realize that my period was late.

Since my period was very regular, almost like a clock, I did not hesitate in buying a pregnancy test. I didn't even have to wait the minutes the pamphlet said: the two lines immediately showed up and I completely broke down in tears.

I must've cried so much that the construction worker came to ask me if I needed anything. It was such a confusing moment that I didn't hesitate in telling him what had happened to me. To my surprise, his reaction was human because he tried to comfort me by saying that maybe a newborn would bring peace to our relationship. That gave me courage, and as soon as he got home, I told him. He was in shock but had the energy to tell me "You're in charge of telling my mom!"

It took me a few days to tell her. I urgently needed to tell her because I couldn't lift heavy stuff at work anymore.

One morning, when we were not working, I confessed it to her. Her response was incredible but she also let me know, for the first time, that Ricardo was not lying to me: "Whaaaat! But how, He told me he doesn't touch you! He does whatever he wants! I see …"

WE WERE BORN TOGETHER

It didn't take long for us to get kicked out of the house. After a few days of prolonged silence, Ricardo told us to leave. I saw him for what he truly was: a monster.

In the stroller, I placed my books (my only possessions), dressed my son, and left.

My mother later received our clothes in total disarray. They delivered them all in a potato sack. What can I say!

Even though many people (including Ricardo) had suggested abortion, I chose to keep the baby with a level of determination that was almost unknown to me.

I turned to all of my options and even took the precaution of joining a healthcare plan. My mother came with me to the ultrasound scan; I remember how nervous she was during the first ultrasound when I was pregnant with my son, but this time it was different. It was peaceful and pleasant.

The doctor told me that I was going to have a girl, which didn't surprise me: something made me think this was going to happen. I was very happy knowing that God was blessing me with two little ones.

My mother insisted I should tell the father, but his tone of contempt held me back every time he would call to ask about his son. I didn't have any intention of letting him know anything about the little one he had clearly rejected in one way or another.

My mother didn't respect my wishes and called Ricardo's mother to tell them about it. Right then and there, he shamelessly called us right back and had the nerve to suggest names for the baby girl.

On October 23, at six-forty in the evening, my daughter was born in the Pereira Rosell Hospital. Only my mother was there with me (the baby's father had visited for ten minutes only two or three times during my hospital stay).

They had to do a Cesarean because I suffered from preeclampsia, (which is transmitted by the man, according to what they told me, and they warned me about the dangers of having multiple pregnancies with the same partner).

I will explain further so that everyone can understand what this disease is. In an article on the Internet, I found the following definition for preeclampsia: "preeclampsia is a disorder that is characterized by high blood pressure during pregnancy, which can cause complications that can affect the fetus just as much as the mother."

The main complication that the mother's high blood pressure can lead to is an increased risk of premature birth, which causes the fetus to be born before completing its growth and development.

This condition presents itself most often in women during their first pregnancy, especially if they are twenty-eight or younger or forty or older. Factors like the presence of diabetes, high blood pressure, anemia, or having family members with hypertension can increase the risk of developing preeclampsia.

I had myself admitted to the hospital about ten days earlier for this reason, but I always felt protected by the other pregnant women as well as the doctors and nurses whom I am still thankful for because of their help in maintaining my physical and emotional well-being.

After being discharged, we went to live in my parents' house; cramped and in poor conditions, but it didn't matter.

My grandmother helped me a lot, taking care of my little baby girl and also trying to make us feel comfortable, and I will always be thankful for her.

In time, I found work, but the pay was not enough to become fully independent. I kept searching, and eventually, I found something better that allowed me to rent a small house, which was good enough for both me and my children. Ever since that day, everything got better.

UNDERSTANDING, DOES IT HELP US TO FORGIVE?

The moment my daughter appeared in the world felt like a soothing breeze from Heaven, an extraordinary breath of Life.

I felt as if I had the energy of a warrior, like the ancient ones we all imagine, capable of facing terrible beasts and the rocky terrains of solitude. A Warrior indeed, and I still am.

Over the years I have had to face the monsters of everyday life.

I started working for a ball-bearing importer. While there, I met my great friend, my Jewish brother, as I like to call him, a very mystical man; medium height, blonde, with green eyes. Thanks to him I was introduced to the personal stories of Second World War survivors. His grandmother was a survivor and came here after the war; walking down our main avenue, she asked a policeman something, and since he treated her so well, she decided to stay in Uruguay.

Much has been published about the Holocaust, a complicated subject, I know, but what better than to know first-hand the horrors suffered by these people? I read as much as I can about this resistance.

My friend once recommended that I read *Many Lives, Many Masters* by Brian Weiss. I finished it in two days, I think, because it completely spoke to me.

Then I got all his books. That reading led me to a world I didn't even know existed. While I had heard about stories of past lives, I never assumed I would be so interested.

Then I discovered the world of The Akashic records. I had to do a bit of research and studying on the internet and in books to thoroughly understand what the Akashic records are. At the beginning, I basically understood that it is like the journey of your soul, life after life, and that the packaging (that is, your body) changes, but the soul is always the same. Here is a definition so that I can clarify this concept a little more: "The Akashic Records are a universal memory of existence, a multidimensional space where all the experiences of the soul are archived including all the knowledge and experiences of past lives, present life and future lives."

This energy system contains all the possibilities that the Soul possesses for its evolution in this life and its true reason for being, the meaning of existence. It is through the connection with our Higher Self, the inner Goddess and the Spirit Guides that we connect to the plane of the Akashic Records in order to heal the Soul, to find the answers to the deepest questions Human Beings have. It caught my attention so much that I decided to look for a record reading specialist.

We met on a Saturday morning at the Zoo. She was already waiting for me. She only knew my name and date of birth.

With her eyes closed, she described to me what she saw, images of a past life of mine: During the Middle Ages, I was very beautiful and was married to a man who mistreated me and took me away from my family and friends; people didn't see me anymore and were slowly forgetting about me. My husband would lock me up and leave me alone. I couldn't stand the abuse anymore so I killed myself.

She continued with her eyes closed and told me that the soul of that medieval man was the same as the man who did the same to me in this life, that I had already fulfilled my purpose here because I had avoided suicide.

At the end of the session, I couldn't stop crying. That woman could not possibly have known the life I have lived being Silvana, because I had never discussed it with anyone.

I felt like screaming, "Now I understand why this happened to me! Now I understand why this happened to me."

I returned home with the answer I had sought after so much, and above all, with the feeling that, because I now understood everything, I could forgive. Forgive every humiliation, every blow, every situation that came so close to death.

Now I struggle to think about whether forgiving means forgetting. Because, I can't forget; forgetting would erase my pain but the pain is still here, in me; it still runs freely down my cheeks.

I have told you my story from the very place you may be in right now: from fear. Because to testify is to relive the horrors; it is to become the living dead.

One thing is very clear, that neither the jealousy, nor the shoving, nor the slightest insult should be accepted. That is not love. That is something I will teach my daughter. But for now, I ask all women, absolutely all of them, not to stay with someone capable of slapping, insulting, humiliating them, or making a big deal out of wearing a short skirt or tight jeans.

I ask everyone in general but also everyone in particular; maybe there is someone reading this, a Mary reading this, or a Claudia, or an Alice, or a Martha or a Sonia, or an Elizabeth, or a Silvia, Naomi, Anna, Emily … please girls, today there are so many more ways to report domestic violence, we have police stations purposely created to defend women, and a toll-free number. A police report can be made anonymously.

Remember that many state agents have to take action if you are not silent: the Justice Department, the Police, the media, educational institutions, medical centers … You will no longer receive the verdict that "The blows are not fresh," which is what unfortunately happened to me years ago. Nothing worse than what you have already endured can happen to you. Remember that I had an unforeseen opportunity when that policeman—that I can't thank enough—fulfilled his professional, civil, and humanitarian duty.

Denounce and defend your right to Live. Denounce and support your survival; and if you still do not feel strong enough to denounce it, do not hesitate to reach out to me. But, please, life is sacred, only God or the Divinity you believe in can take us when the time comes, not a coward who abuses us; DENOUNCE!

Do it for all the women who have been murdered, for all the women we have resurrected, and for Yourself, as we are all a part of You.

ABOUT THE AUTHOR

Silvana Marconi is a Uruguayan author born in Montevideo in 1977. She teaches English, is married, and has two teenage kids. She is a former victim of domestic violence. She is the author of Sobreviví, published in 2018. She has published a second book Mi historia de amor con un ex preso de Guantánamo and is currently working on her third book about parental alienation. She likes to write about real stories, and those are the types of books she prefers to read. She is currently working with two producers on a documentary about domestic violence. (Link to raise money through IDEAME, Latin America's crowdfunding, for the post production of the documentary).

Through this book she tells her story of survival and denounces her aggressor. Following in her footsteps, many other Uruguayan women built up the courage to report their aggressors and have used Silvana's book as a point of reference. She has numerous followers on social media and has been a guest in various television and radio shows, creating awareness on this very important and impactful topic.

ABOUT THE TRANSLATORS

D r. Biasetti is an Associate Professor of Spanish in the Department of English and World Languages at Augusta University and is specialized in teaching all levels of Spanish, Translation, and Literature. She is the Director of the Salamanca, Spain Study Abroad Program. Dr. Biasetti is Italian, but born in Lima, Perú. She lived in Perú (Lima), Venezuela (Caracas), Italy (Milan), and the United States (Florida, Iowa, and Georgia).

- Students in SPAN 4600 (Introduction to Spanish— English Translation):
  - Sasha Bent (Spanish and Psychology Major and Linguistics Minor)
  - Steven Boyd (Spanish Major and Linguistics Minor)

- Stephanie Castillo (Pre-Social Work Major and Spanish Minor)
- Julio Chavez (Chemistry Major and Spanish Minor)
- Emilee Kirby (Undeclared, Nursing Major and Spanish Minor)
- Lakshminaga Sai Srut Medicherla (Biology Major and Spanish Minor)
- Carragan Moody (Undeclared, Nursing Major and Spanish Minor)
- Francesca Santander (Cell & Molecular Biology Major and Spanish Minor)
- Tania Satizabal (Undeclared, Nursing Major and Spanish Minor)
- Hollie Swanson (Spanish Major and French Minor)
- Nathan Urioste (Communication Major and Accounting and Spanish Minor)